Andrew Plant

Could a Tyrannosaurus Play Table Tennis?

Kane Miller
A DIVISION OF EDC PUBLISHING

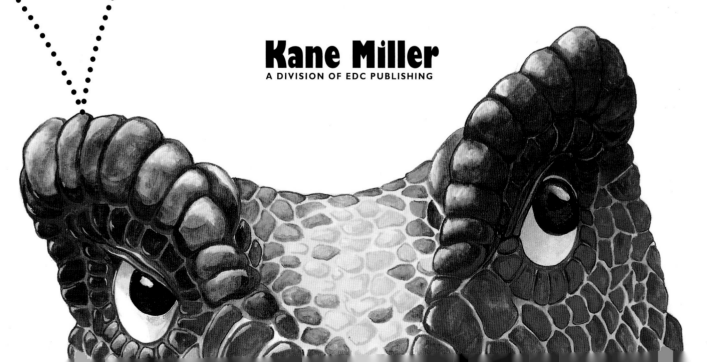

One reason why dinosaurs are so fascinating to so many people is that some of them were big. Not just *"Gee, you've put on some weight,"* big, or even *"Wow, that's really big,"* big. The really big dinosaurs were *"You've got to be kidding!"* big. But saying that something was 98 feet long or 52 feet high or weighed over 55 tons doesn't really get the idea across – they're just numbers. So, what if we say something was longer than a basketball court? Or taller than the tallest pole vault? Or had feet as big as a kettle drum? Comparisons always help, and not just when things are big. Some dinosaurs were really small – no longer than a dog – just as interesting as the big ones, and easier to keep in the backyard!

In this book, you'll find all sorts of dinosaurs – from nearly the biggest to just about the smallest. Some are really famous and have been known about for decades. Others have only been discovered in the last few years. I've painted them all to scale in relation to the things around them, whether it's a golf club, a table tennis table, or a basketball court. Some things, like ice, or a circus ball, may not give you as much of an idea about size though, so look at the big parade picture at the back of the book for comparisons. Every dinosaur in the book is there, at just the right size.

Also, at the bottom of each page, I've added some extra information – what period the dinosaur lived in, where its fossils were found, how big it was, and what it ate. If you want to find out even more, there are lots of good books around, or you could search the internet.

One thing we will never know is what color the dinosaurs were. Dinosaurs evolved from primitive reptiles (not lizards, by the way, even though "dinosaur" means "terrible lizard"), and birds evolved from one group of the dinosaurs. Many reptiles and many birds are brightly colored, sometimes for camouflage, sometimes for display. It's very likely some dinosaurs too, were brightly colored. For fun, I've made all the dinosaurs in this book pretty colorful. (It's actually very unlikely that they all would have been so bright, but a few of them probably were.) Whatever color they were, we can be sure that, when alive, they were amazing and wonderful animals. What wouldn't I give to be able to go back to the Age of the Dinosaurs – just for one day?

To Pat V.-R.
for inspiration

To Bron
for everything

First American Edition 2006
Kane/Miller Book Publishers, Inc.,
La Jolla, California

First published by Penguin Books Australia, 2002
Copyright © Andrew Plant, 2002

Library of Congress Control Number: 2005930586
Printed and bound in China by Regent Publishing Services, Ltd.
2 3 4 5 6 7 8 9 10
ISBN: 978-1-929132-97-3

Look at all these dinosaurs!
I wonder what they could do?

A

AN-Ki-SERRA-tops
close horned face

Could an Anchiceratops be an acrobat?

Cretaceous   North America   17 ft long   herbivore

Could a Brachiosaurus play basketball?

BRAK-ee-oh-SORE-us
arm lizard

Jurassic and Cretaceous | North America, Africa | 82 ft long, 52 ft high, 33–56 tons | herbivore

C

Could a **Carnotaurus** play cricket?

KAR-noh-TORE-us
meat-eating bull

Could a Deinonychus go dancing?

D

die-NON-i-kus
terrible claw

E

ed-mon-TONE-ee-a
from Edmonton

Could an Edmontonia hold an exhibition?

Could a Fabrosaurus go fishing?

FAB-roh-SORE-us
Fabre's lizard

Jurassic Africa 3 ft long herbivore

G

GAL-lee-MEEM-us
fowl mimic

Could a Gallimimus
play golf?

Could a **Homalocephale** play field hockey?

H

HOME-ah-loh-SEF-ah-lee
even head

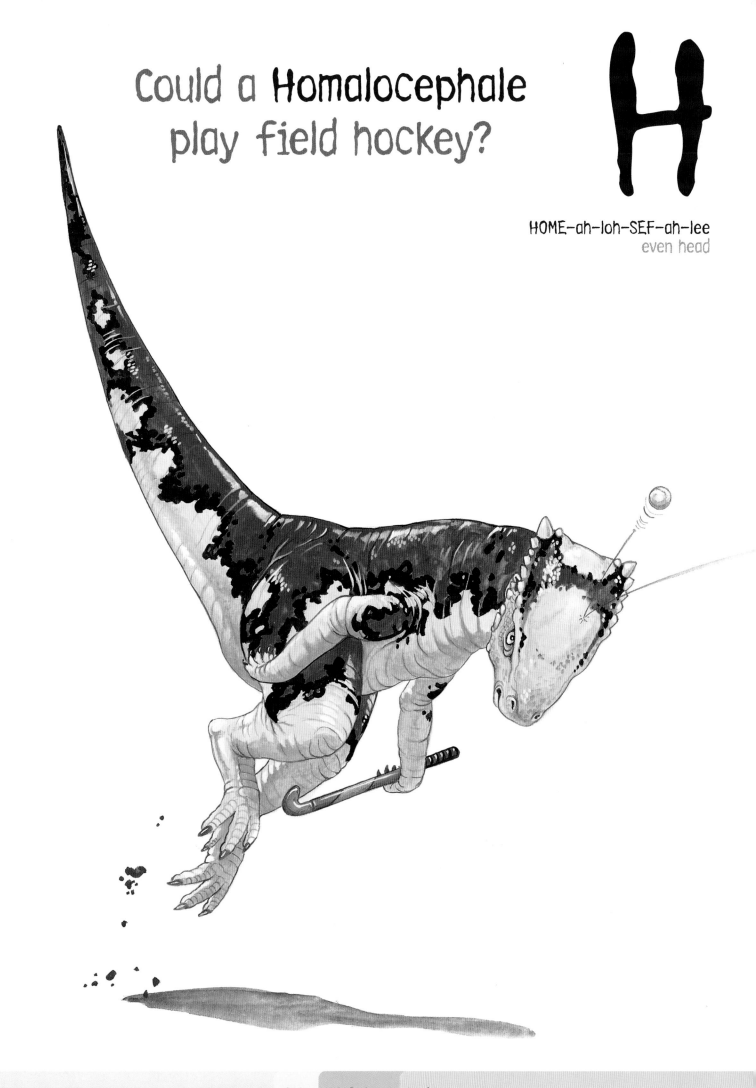

Cretaceous   Asia   10 ft long   herbivore

I

Could an Iguanodon ice skate?

i-GWHA-noh-don
iguana tooth

Could a **Jaxartosaurus** juggle?

J

jak-SART-oh-SORE-us
Jaxartes lizard

Cretaceous   Asia   30 ft long   herbivore

Could a Kentrosaurus fly a kite?

KEN-troh-SORE-us
sharp-point lizard

Jurassic   Africa   17 ft long   herbivore

Could a Lambeosaurus do the limbo?

LAM-bee-oh-SORE-us
Lambe's lizard

Cretaceous　North America　49 ft　herbivore

M

Could a Mamenchisaurus play music?

mah-MEN-chee-SORE-us
Mamenchi lizard

Could a Neovenator play netball?

neo-ve-NAY-tor
new hunter

Cretaceous Europe 26 ft carnivore

O

oo-RAHN-oh-SORE-us
brave monitor lizard

Could an Ouranosaurus sing opera?

Could a Parasaurolophus pole vault?

P

par-a-sore-oh-LOH-fus
beside ridged lizard

Cretaceous   North America   33 ft long   herbivore

Q

KWON—tah—SORE—us
Qantas lizard

Could a Qantassaurus play quoits?

Cretaceous Australia 6 ft long herbivore

Could a Rhoetosaurus go rowing?

REET–oh–SORE–us
Rhoetos lizard

Jurassic   Australia   49 ft long   herbivore

S

Could a Styracosaurus play soccer?

sty-RAK-oh-SORE-us
spiked lizard

Could a Tyrannosaurus play table tennis?

ti-RAN-oh-SORE-us
tyrant lizard

U

oon-en-LAHG-ee-a
half bird

Could an Unenlagia play underwater hockey?

Could a Velociraptor play volleyball?

V

vel-O-si-RAP-tor
swift plunderer

Could a Wannanosaurus lift weights?

wan-NAN-oh-SORE-us
Wannan lizard

Cretaceous   Asia   2 ft long   herbivore

Could a **Xuanhanosaurus** take an X-ray?

shwan-HAHN-oh-SORE-us
Xuanhan lizard

Jurassic   Asia   **20 ft long**   carnivore

Could a Yangchuanosaurus go yachting?

yung–CHWUN–oh–SORE–us
Yangchuan lizard

M.S. MINNOW

Could a Zizhongosaurus fly with a zeppelin?

zer-JONG-oh-SORE-us
Zizhong lizard

Jurassic   Asia   30 ft long   herbivore

If we could take one home,
I wonder what he could do...